50 Lessons
for Parents
Before
They Start
Writing Checks

The Truth About College

Will S. Keim

Chalice Press

St. Louis, Missouri

Art Director: Lynne Condellone
Cover design: Michael Dominguez
Illustration: Robert Watkins

10 9 8 7 6 5 4 3 2 1   97 98 99 00 01 02

Library of Congress Cataloging-in-Publication Data

Keim, Will.

The truth about college : 50 lessons for parents before they start writing checks / Will S. Keim.

p.   cm.

ISBN 0-8272-3633-6

1. Universities and colleges—United States.   2. Education, Higher—Aims and objectives—United States.   3. College choice—United States.   4. College student orientation United States.   I. Title.

LA227.4.K45   1997   97-21803
378.73—dc21   CIP

Printed in the United States of America

FOREWORD

Parents view college as an important investment in their child's future. Now, financially, the prospect of that future is eluding many of them. Parents hear about the college parties, the "trappings" of the modern college environment, the lengthened time for degree attainment (in many cases five or six years) and these factors add anger to the frustration of securing college degrees for their sons and daughters.

Along with that scenario, some educational writers are now describing another concomitant phenomenon. Students are becoming consumers, with a keener sense of responsibility to their parents' financial challenges and the need to attain a "no frills," quality education in the shortest possible time. Students' values also appear to be changing, with fewer and fewer willing to spend time partying and imbibing, in the college traditions of the past.

These new parent and student scenarios demand a response, and just in time, Dr. Will Keim produced this book to lead parents and even students through the maze of college selection to college survival through appropriate parental support. The timing of this publication is no surprise to those of us who know Dr. Keim. With his publications, Will seems to have been blessed with the ability to synthesize the important life issues of young people and their families, guiding them all toward enhanced levels of personal fulfillment and satisfaction.

Parents: You may have thought your job was over and that you were no longer needed in your child's life. Depending on your perspective, the good and bad news is that you are needed more than ever.

Dr. Keim's book will lift you up, and make you cry. It will calm your fears, then raise new questions. In whatever way it impacts you, it will lead you through a challenge, then deliver you to a joyous celebration of your child's success as a college student and person. Read *The Truth About College*, do what it says, then rejoice in its revelations and assistance for this important phase of your life.

Ray K. Zarvell
Executive Director of Educational Development
Bradley University

Table of Contents

PART I: COLLEGE SECTION

PART II: PARENT SECTION

PART III: STUDENT SECTION

PART IV: CONCLUDING THOUGHTS

INTRODUCTION

"Always tell the truth; it will amaze half the people and astonish the rest."

Mark Twain

I am a product of the twentieth century university, and I do not intend or desire to bite the hand that has fed me, nurtured me, and raised me up. Neither of my parents attended the university, and my attendance and graduation was a great source of pride for them and me. Still, this book demands to be written. Parents deserve *The Truth About College*. They deserve it because they pay for their children's education or ignorance. Their taxes endow a mighty budget oft directed more by political motive and correctness than by not-so-common sense.

My goal is to strengthen the educational system by creating informed and inquisitive consumers of the product education. The collegiate experience has changed dramatically since most of us were enrolled, and I plan to share the insights I have had during the last ten years while visiting more than eight hundred campuses personally. I have spoken to over two million students, whose wisdom and observations will underscore the need for parental and societal involvement in higher education.

Three basic assumptions guide my motive in writing *The Truth About College:*

1. THE COLLEGIATE EXPERIENCE IS WORTH THE MONEY. If you think education is expensive, try the price of ignorance. You pay for education once, whereas you will pay for ignorance every day for

the rest of your life. The worth, of course, relates directly to attendance and effort of student *and* professor.

2. *IF PARENTS TRULY KNEW WHAT WAS GOING ON, THEY WOULD PAY MORE ATTENTION.* Chapter 6 of the College Section will discuss one area of grave concern. That is, how many of your student's classes are being taught by teaching assistants in lieu of the terminally degreed professionals? Clearly, the more parents know, the more they are going to want to know.

3. *SUPREME COURT JUSTICES AND TENURED PROFESSORS GET JOBS-FOR-LIFE.* Translation: The university can, without public and parental care, concern, and prodding, exist in a vacuum. All institutions, public and private, are in some degree publicly funded, and we pay the rest. Parents must make certain that their children receive up-to-date and -century information and are marketable and hireable upon graduation.

I plan to send my four children to college, provided they desire to go. But I assure you I will ask many questions. *The Truth About College* will reveal to you my joys, concerns, and fears about the collegiate experience.

My promise to you the parent or guardian is this:

If you take the time to read this book, then you will be extremely valuable to your child as he or she learns to succeed in the university world.

You will spend your time and money more wisely.

And...

Your student will benefit from your guidance and have a better chance of graduating and making the transition into life.

The Truth About College is not a cure-all, but it is the truth about college written by a person who has lived and worked on campus and in the world for twenty years; written for parents who still accept their responsibility to care for, love, and encourage their children.

Simply put:

The more time and energy you invest now in preparing yourself and your student for the experience, the less time you will spend after drop-out or graduation with an ill-prepared or unprepared, and very unhappy, young person.

Choose *now* as the time to invest!

PART I

COLLEGE
SECTION

The Philosophy of
Higher Education:

The Education of Character

"Education worthy of the name is essentially the education of character."

Martin Buber

There was a time not long ago when learned people were expected to know everything there was to know about their subject. It must be noted that this concept preceded computers, CNN, Bill Gates, and several other individuals and institutions of the Information Age. Tom Peters proposes that the information in the world doubles every three years, and the Internet is the Gutenberg Press to the Infinite Power of forever. The purpose of higher education was to pass on the accrued knowledge to the next generation. Now the information passes free from the Web browser to the individual, so we must ask: What is the purpose, the philosophy, the raison d'être for the university?

As a parent, you should ask the college or university for the following information:

1. The institution's philosophy of higher education.

2. A mission statement.

3. Goals and objectives and projected student-oriented outcomes.

4. The actual in-class and office hours required of the faculty.

5. Publication and consulting records for faculty in your student's field of study.

It is true that your child will work in fields perhaps not yet invented, so how can the college prepare your child for a career in _____?

At the same time, a meaningful philosophy of education, a strong desire to teach, a competent faculty and staff, a safe campus, and an institutional commitment to quality will greatly enhance the chances for your student's success.

I am most concerned about what kind of person your child will be encouraged to become at the university. The content of his or her character is paramount. If your student becomes a doctor or lawyer without a well-developed sense of ethics, then what have we accomplished? Who has won?

Find a campus that openly talks about character and teaches and programs toward its development, and you will have found a starting place built on a strong foundation.

Professional education and vocational training are very important. The education of character develops life skills for the creation of a meaningful and enjoyable life lived in genuine community with others. What could be more important?

The American Council
on Education:

The Value of a College Degree

"If you think the price of education is expensive, try the price of ignorance. You pay for ignorance everyday for the rest of your life."

Anonymous

As college costs continue to grow at rates exceeding inflation, parents wonder about the real value of a college education. It is clear that a person can enjoy success, financial or otherwise, without necessarily completing a degree program. For a moment, and putting the "education of character" argument presented in chapter 1 aside, what is the real value of a college degree?

A recent study published in *USA Today* reporting on an American Council on Education study documented an average degree-holder gain of over six hundred thousand lifetime dollars above the high school-educated worker. This is the bottom line. I believe a stronger case can be made for character development, life enrichment, ability to work collaboratively and in diverse community, and personal enrichment. But on a purely financial basis the rewards of a degree are substantial. It should be noted too that a professional degree-holder, M.B.A., Ph.D., J.D., M.D., etc., on the average will make four to five times the monthly income of the person without degree preparation. Education is expensive but pales in comparison to the cost of ignorance.

One colleague remarked to me, "You know, it costs more money to send someone to the State Pen than it does to send them to Penn State." Frontloading the investment in education is a positive first step toward personal satisfaction and happiness.

And as Jefferson so aptly posited, "A nation's best defense is an educated citizenry." If you think the price of education is expensive, try the price of ignorance. You pay for education once. You pay for ignorance every day the rest of your life.

Choosing the Right Campus:

The Student-Environment Fit

"Be more concerned with your character than your reputation. Your character is what you really are while your reputation is merely what others think you are."

John Wooden

Have you seen a college catalog where the days are not bright blue with sunshine-filled skies? Where women students gaze apprehensively over their shoulder, straining to see what that noise was in poor pathway lighting? Are there pictures of hour-long registration lines each term because the university won't computerize registration? Did you read the section on the crime statistics for the campus and surrounding community? Will the campus grounds be accessible to your wheelchair-bound student?

There are dozens of criteria that go into selecting a campus that provides a good student-environment fit. To begin the search for the campus best suited for your student:

1. *TALK TO EACH OTHER.* Find out what academic or vocational interests your child is thinking about. *Not your interests...*your student's interests. You did not appreciate your parents attempting to run your life. Then why do the same thing to your children?

2. *DISCUSS COSTS.* I went to a private school my parents could not afford because I could throw a curve ball. What is your financial picture? Scholarship potential? There are hundreds of scholarships never applied for because of ignorance of their existence. *Talk to your child's guidance counselor for information.* Don't be deluded by seemingly large scholarships at high-tuition institutions. A twenty-thousand-dollar scholarship at a thirty-thousand-dollar-a-year campus still leaves a healthy chunk of change to pay. Be honest about your financial ability.

3. *DO READ THE CATALOG,* but remember the four-color brochure for the Titanic looked beautiful too! If you have any questions or need clarification, call the registrar or admissions office for assistance.

4. *VISIT CAMPUS.* Take an official tour through the admissions office, preferably with a student host. Sit in on a class, meet the Dean of Students, walk through the recreation center. Then, check it out at night. The days and nights of campus civility and safety are over in most places. Do you feel safe at night? Is the campus well-lit? Finally, go into the library to see if it is up-to-date and utilized. Talk to students leaving the library about the campus, its academics, and student life. Students will be candid and brutally honest most of the time.

5. *ASK FOR A LIST OF ALUMNI IN YOUR AREA* whom you and your student can visit. If the university does not track this information, then there is a reason (and a problem). Alumni can help you assess the campus and the value of its degree for them.

I attended the University of the Pacific, which was perfect for my needs with its small, personal emphasis on teaching for undergraduate education. My Ph.D. was completed at Oregon State University, a major land, sea, and space grant research institution. The student-environment fit is an essential piece in the college success puzzle. Information is power: the power to make good choices based on knowledge of self and situation. Do your homework! Find a college with character whose reality equals its reputation.

The Campus Environment:
This Is Reality

"You are setting the banquet table at the university for the feast you will eat the rest of your life."

Will Keim

Many students have told me that they will get serious when they get to the "real world." When I ask them where they think the real world is located and when it begins, they report that the "real world" is after college.

On the contrary, college is part of real life. Patterns established in school often accompany the graduate into the rest of real life called employment or graduate school. Jim Matthews of Keene State College in New Hampshire, for example, has documented that fifty percent of all students who drink heavily will continue to do so during their immediate post-college years. This is often a time of tremendous learning and relearning where a base is built for career advancement and enhancement.

> *The Point:* College choices and behaviors are real and directly related to choices, consequences, and opportunities (or lack thereof) after graduation.

Campus life may at times seem light years away from reality, but the choices made as an undergraduate, even as a freshman or new student, will directly impact the number of options from which the student later has to choose.

- Once the grade point average falls below 1.0 during the first year, all subsequent academic excellence will be tarnished by its accumulative effect on the overall G.P.A.

- A possessions charge for marijuana use can result in a felony, not a misdemeanor, under the 1990 Drug Free Campus and Community Act. Companies now check records and do drug testing.

- A racial taunt viewed 20 years ago as insensitive and ignored may now be prosecuted under a state's Hate Law ordinances and statutes.

Life on campus is real and is the stage upon which all subsequent actions will occur. It should be taken seriously, enjoyed, and used as a time to prepare academically, socially, and spiritually for the journey into the rest of real life after college. Students who know this do well. Students who ignore this reality often move home with their mommies and daddies, failing to set the banquet table for the feast life holds for them.

The Faculty:

Teaching, Research, and Service

"Education, whether for success or failure, is never finished. Building and sustaining the settings in which individuals can grow and unfold, not 'kept in their place' but empowered to become all they can be, is not only the task of parents and teachers, but the basis of management and political leadership and simple friendship."

Mary Catherine Bateson

Five years ago I was a lot more judgmental and angry with faculty members than I am today. Why? Because in all things these days in my life I see increasing shades of gray and much less black and white. Is that called middle-age?

It has become clear to me that most faculty members are rewarded with promotion and tenure for research, publication, and an emerging third factor, securing outside grant monies. These three activities bring honor and prestige to departments and universities. Rare is the professor who is promoted and tenured for pure excellence in teaching and service to students and community. Some examples:

- A Business professor is denied tenure for lack of scholarly production despite having written a 400-page application of technology model for IBM. Reason? In the university's promotion calculations, his manual counts the same as a one-page paper presented at a national conference.

  He sadly leaves his $36,000 a year job he loves for a $90,000 a year job with IBM. He loses, and so does your student.

- A Faculty Committee votes 40–5 to tenure an English professor, only to have a five-man committee reverse the decision because their department has too many tenured faculty. The denial has nothing to do with competence or teaching but reveals a Senior Faculty entrenched in lifelong jobs.

You must research the faculty at the university and ask some good questions:

1. Have the Business faculty ever been in business? Even if they have failed in business, they will have learned greatly from the experience. Have they been on the battlefield?

2. Have the English faculty written anything after their dissertations?

3. Does the Agriculture School have any farmers on the faculty?

Not all knowledge is experiential, but neither is it all book-learning. Does the university mix theoreticians with practitioners? How are the faculty rewarded? Does serving and teaching your student fit into the promotion/tenure equation at all?

Seek and solicit faculty who are committed to knowledge and its teaching to students; men and women who want to mentor the next generation of leaders. Finally, tell your student to share with you a list of class and office hours for each of his or her professors. This will be instructive.

Education, like your "job" as a parent, is never finished.

The B.A., The T.A., and The M.A.:

The Way Teaching Is Done

"All is not cream that comes from a cow."

Yiddish Proverb

What I am about to say is a generalization of the way teaching is done. My description is especially not applicable at small private universities and colleges where emphasis is normally placed on teaching excellence and strong faculty-student relationships— colleges like Bates, Carleton, Davidson, University of Missouri (a state university by the way!). At these and other campuses, you could expect the finest in the art of teaching. But all is not cream that comes from a cow, in fact some is plain c__p!

It is not unusual to have a well-intentioned B.A. (someone with a bachelor's degree) who is a T.A. (a teaching assistant) pursuing an M.A. (the master's degree) doing a lot of the teaching, especially at the undergraduate, freshman, or new student 100-level (entry) classes. I challenge any university administrator to dispute this contention.

Now mind you, when I taught at Oregon State University, I was a T.A. and was rated by over four thousand students as Outstanding Professor of the Year. I already had an M.A. in Speech Communication, however, and was finishing a Ph.D. Several of my "colleagues" were B.A.s working on M.A.s, and I believe they did an excellent job of teaching.

Here is my point:
Would you expect to pay the same amount of money to see the San Francisco 49ers play football as you would Stanford University? And Stanford would cost more than St. Ignatius High School, wouldn't it? We're talking professional and amateur, quality and experience.

Why then would you pay the same tuition for a tenured Ph.D. as you would the B.A. who is the T.A. seeking the M.A.? If you say it doesn't matter, if you contend that the T.A.s do just as good a job as the Ph.D.s, then I could show you some sure ways to save lots of money in salary and benefit packages.

Ask the tough questions:

- How many of my daughter's classes will be taught directly by terminally degreed (Ph.D., Ed.D., J.D., M.D., etc.) professionals?

- What is the faculty/student ratio, not counting graduate students, especially in entry-level required courses?

- How many office hours do the faculty keep each week? The T.A.s?

When it comes to your child's education, you want the cream of the crop!

The Dean of Students:

A Human Resource
for Co-Curricular Activities

*"A university should be a place of light,
of liberty, of learning."*

Benjamin Disraeli

The university or college terms those things that happen in the classroom or the research laboratory as "academic" or curricular. Sadly, most institutions still hold to the outdated and misnomer "extracurricular" for those things that occur outside the classroom. Using this unfortunate and inaccurate labeling, some "extracurricular activities" might include:

- Intramurals

- Interest clubs

- Student government

but also,

- Study skills seminars

- Resume writing workshops

- Health and wellness aerobic classes through the campus recreation center

The point is this:

My experience has taught me that your student may learn just as much or more from these so-called "extra-curricular activities" as with the "curricular" ones.

What is "extra..." about your child being physically and spiritually fit, with good writing and speaking skills, being able to work cooperatively with others toward the achievement of a mutually agreed-upon goal, with leadership experiences, and having a solid resume?

All of these factors can often be better learned in the more relaxed atmosphere of what we will hereafter call:

Co-Curricular Activities...

...In the classroom activities? Not often. Essential? Only to those students who will succeed in making the transition from college to life.

Curricular and co-curricular. Two parts to the whole of university and college life. Quality colleges know this and take both parts seriously. They involve students in a myriad of experiences that develop the whole person, not just the intellectual dimension.

The Dean of Students and the Vice President or Provost for Student Services, Student Development, or on some campuses, Student Personnel are key players in the co-curricular side of university life. Meet the dean or vice president on your campus visit. You should sense a person deeply committed to the development of young men and women, a person who understands the emotional and intellectual development of college-age and nontraditional students.

I have yet to see, in over 800 campus visits, a university or college with great campus life that doesn't have a good dean or vice president. If the dean is distant and distracted, what would make you think the Division of Student Affairs would be any different? Check out the dean, ask for her or his philosophy of co-curricular activities, ask students on campus if they know who the Dean of Students or Vice President of Student Life is, and then you will catch a glimpse of campus life. Remember, 70 percent of your student's time will be spent outside of the classroom in what we know to be co-curricular activities.

A university is much more than in-classroom instruction!

The Health Educator:

A Friend in Need

"When choosing between two evils, J always like to try the one J've never tried before."

Mae West

One of the most important co-curricular areas is the health educator's office. Years ago this generally was a nurse who patched wounds and offered comfort. It was important then and vital today. Why?

The professional health educator today is at times a nurse, doctor, or especially trained professional who is arguably the best person to educate students about AIDS, sexually transmitted diseases, alcohol and drug abuse, stress, and a host of other life-altering and -threatening issues.

Health educators teach co-curricular classes, write columns for campus newspapers, counsel and advise students individually, and serve as unofficial ombudsmen for student health and wellness. They are perceived as objective and fair, and since few if any have any disciplinary responsibilities, students can confide in them without fear of recrimination, judgment, or punishment.

This said, can you imagine a good reason for a campus not to have a health educator? I cannot. It is a high-priority area and merits a strong commitment from administration and faculty. Visit the campus health center, find out if its services are included in tuition or fees, and meet the health educator. He or she may be the person your student turns to in time of need.

When Mae West made her famous joke about untried evil, there were not as many mistakes that could kill as there are today. There were fewer mistakes that could show up on your resumé or credit report, thanks to technology. The "stakes of mistakes" are immense today. The health educator is one more line of defense toward the goal of moving students into and through the university and out into productive participation in society by taking responsibility for their own lives. Education should prepare them to educate themselves in a lifelong love of learning.

The Resident Assistant:

The Front Line of Concern

"No one has yet fully realized the wealth of sympathy, kindness and generosity hidden in the soul of a child. The effort of every true education should be to unlock that treasure."

Emma Goldman

N ot every student will live in a college or university residence hall. Finances dictate home stay for some students, and commuters generally brave two worlds: the campus and the workplace worlds.

Resident Assistants or Advisors are generally undergraduate peers who have been selected by the professional Residential Life staff to live and work among the student residents. They receive training in:

- Communication skills
- Conflict resolution
- Diversity issues
- First aid
- Programming
  ...and many other areas.

They serve to enforce university and hall policies and submit maintenance request forms to keep the hall in good operating order. They are then responsible for the educational, cultural, social, and recreational programming on a floor within a hall, as well as policy enforcement and conflict resolution.

They will see your student more than any other person on campus and can be a fabulous resource should you be unable to reach your child or be concerned with safety, academic, or health concerns. There is a limit to what they can or will tell you (see chapter 12), but they are sincerely interested in and concerned about their residents and your child. The Resident Assistant may hold some very important keys to unlocking the mystery that is the university and the mystery that is your student. The R.A. is the frontline of concern, care, and help.

The Two-Year and the Four-Year Schools:

Plumbers and Doctors Side By Side

"The desk is a dangerous place from which to watch the world."

John Le Carré

There is a great mythology in the world that leads us to believe that one needs a college education to get a job, find meaning in life, and be a good person. We speak glowingly of college-bound high school students and feel sorry for those parents whose children consider community college, the military, or (gasp) employment.

Bunk! I am a strong advocate and supporter of education, but students can learn, or choose not to learn, at a four- or two-year college, or in job situations. It is time for our nation to validate in-classroom and out-of-classroom education. There are business professors at top schools who couldn't run a business and successful entrepreneurs who could be the Dean of the Graduate School of Business. The "teacher" can take many forms, but the willingness of the "student" to learn is absolutely essential.

Fred Smith's plan for Federal Express, for example, was poorly graded as a senior thesis, but it sure works if it absolutely, positively has to be there by the next morning. You can practically hear the professor saying, with a knowing smirk, "Let me get this straight, Mr. Smith... you are going to ship all the packages to Memphis, Tennessee, first, then fly them out from there...right?" "Bad" academics...great business! The Post Office is just now starting to recover from the shock. How do you think the professor feels about this former student's project?

It was an expert in higher education that saved Albertson's College of Idaho. It was a furniture mogul with a B.A. and a man who convinced us that "It's Joe Albertson's Super Market, but the produce department is mine!"

I am not minimizing professionals in higher education or the collegiate experience. My life would be vastly different and much poorer without the University of the Pacific, Oregon State University, and professors like Ed Bryan, Don Duns, Tom Ambrogi, Judy Chambers, JoAnne Trow, Mike Beachley, and Marcus Borg! What I am calling to your attention is that good people and successful people take different paths.

Allowing or encouraging your child to experience the "joy" of the fifty-hour work week today might just make him or her a great student one year from now.

And quite seriously...the plumbers can and do live next door to the doctors. And who is to say that a happy salesclerk or assistant cook is any worse off than a lawyer who hates her practice? If money made people happy, then North America would be blissful. Rather, we spend 59 billion dollars a year on alcohol and import 150 metric tons of cocaine. Go figure!

The university is only one place of many where education takes place.

The desk, like the sink drain, is not for everyone!

Public and Private Institutions:

Making a Sound Investment

"The great lesson from the true mystics...is that the sacred is in the ordinary, that it is to be found in one's daily life, in one's neighbors, friends, and family, in one's backyard."

Abraham Maslow

There is certain mystique in America regarding a private education that motivates some people to do whatever it takes to pay at times over $20,000 a year in tuition alone for an education, when in reality the student may or may not attend class regularly. This private school fixation fits in with America's tendency to pay an amazing amount of attention to members of the United Kingdom's Royal Family, when just two centuries ago we overthrew the yoke of English rule. We at times desire democracy and justice...it just seems as if those with the most money get a little bit more justice and a bigger slice of the democratic pie. This is even more interesting when you consider that Canada, though having the Queen on a lot of its money, has very few private institutions, while maintaining a very public education system.

I attended a private undergraduate institution because I could throw a curve ball and received partial financial aid. I loved it! I knew every professor personally, I attended social and educational functions in their homes, they attended my wedding, and I had values and ethics laced into nearly every class. It was clear at the University of The Pacific that they were concerned with the character of the graduates as well as their employability and cultural literacy. UOP was the third-highest-priced university in the country then. I was lucky to go there.

My graduate work was at Oregon State University, where the resources of a land, space, and sea grant university could not be approached by the small private school. Great research and community service projects, tremendous grant securement, and a huge faculty made the campus a dynamic place that was very exciting for me at the graduate level in the Pacific-10 Conference.

Here are some suggestions as you and the student choose the institution, public or private:

1. IDENTIFY YOUR MOTIVES. Why do you desire to send your child to a private school? Is it better? How so? Do you think the education is markedly better, or do you believe your student will be associated with a different or "better" class of student? What does this tell you about yourself and your values? Complete a pro and con list for public and private schools.

2. WHAT PERCENTAGE OF ENTRY-LEVEL CLASSES ARE TAUGHT BY PH.D.'S OR TERMINAL DEGREE HOLDERS (i.e. J.D., M.D., C.P.A., etc.?) This is an area where the private schools usually hold the edge. There is a huge dropout problem after the first year of college life. Will your student be receiving the kind of instruction that will make him or her want to return to the university?

3. CAN YOU AFFORD IT? CAN YOUR STUDENT AFFORD IT? Be really careful as you look at financial aid packages. Grants mean something akin to scholarships, work-study means you work for the cash on campus, loans are loans. Dissect the package and ask yourselves, "Is this education worth being $40,000+ in debt at the end of four to five years?"

4. WOULD THE MONEY BE BETTER SPENT ON PRIVATE HIGH SCHOOL EDUCATION? Take a look at the gap between private and public college education, and then look at the gap in your area

between private and public high school education. Where would your money be best spent?

5. ARE THE GRADUATES GETTING JOBS OR INTO GRADUATE SCHOOL? I would never encourage my children to attend any school that considered employment beneath their concerns. This applies to both private and public institutions.

My first two years at the private institution were not well spent because I did not apply myself. The last two years, I attended every class and read every assignment, and it was a wonderful time of personal growth and preparation. At the public institution, I received a quality education, but it was clearly less personal than the private school.

What does your student need? What can you afford? What is your motivation? I would have been lost at a big school, so UOP was perfect for me. Graduate school was different. Most quality schools will be able to tell you exactly the placement rate of graduates in the workforce and in graduate school. What could be an institution's motivation in not keeping those statistics? Think about it...and make a wise investment!

No university, from the most prestigious private school to the public state university, can educate a student who does not want to learn, won't show up, and isn't motivated. To me, the institution is less important than the attitude of the learner...*your student!*

The Freedom of Information Act:

What You Can and Cannot Know

"Complacency is a far more dangerous attitude than outrage."

Naomi Little Bear

T wo of my favorite deans in higher education are Bruce Pitman of the University of Idaho and Charlotte Burgess of the University of Redlands. Both of these highly skilled and caring professionals love students, work well collaboratively, and would be someone I would be thrilled to have in a mentoring role with my children.

Both Dean Pitman and Dean Burgess wrestle with the Freedom of Information Act because they know it "takes a whole village to raise a child." The problem centers on what these deans and their colleagues can tell you about your student and what they cannot tell you.

If all parents, like you, cared enough to read a book about their student's collegiate experience, then this would be a smaller problem. Unfortunately, some parents berate their children, rape their children, beat their children, and try to dominate and control their children's lives. It is for these parents and for the freedom and rights of all young adults that I believe the Freedom of Information Act exists.

Simply put, students can, within reason, control what information the university gives you about them. So, have or develop a relationship of trust, be a good and nonjudgmental listener, and you will be rewarded with a flow of information from your child that keeps you on the right page.

Do not be complacent! It is, in my opinion as a parent and as an educator, your job to know:

- How your child can be reached in an emergency.

- Where he or she is living.

- What your child's major is and what year he or she is in school.

Would you believe me if I told you that a set of parents, good people, traveled several thousand miles to witness their son's graduation, only to find out he was in credit-hours a second-semester freshman after four years? It is true! They wrote checks for four years for a paid vacation for their irresponsible offspring. Please do not laugh at them. They committed the sin of complacency and blind trust.

The key is to check up but not let the student see your checking as anything other than love, concern, and maybe at worst parental good-natured meddling. Establish a good relationship with your dean, who will tell you as much as he or she can.

P.S. What I enjoy most about Charlotte Burgess is her ability to set high standards for students and still be a mentor and friend to them. Bruce Pitman gives the parents his home phone number. You cannot get more accessible than that!

Know the Freedom of Information Act and keep the lines of communication open weekly with your student.

Complacency is a far more dangerous attitude than having your children think you want to know too much. You can always back off a little. Be clear that the stakes of student's mistakes are enormous. Love them, teach them, then let them fly. Be close by should they need help. It is what all the other species do! Maybe we humans should give it a try.

PART II

PARENT
SECTION

The Reality of Parenthood:
Is This the Little One I Carried?

"I have found the best way to give advice to your children is to find out what they want and then advise them to do it."

Harry S. Truman

Recently I gave the commencement address at the graduation ceremonies at Eastern Connecticut State University. The biggest response of the scorching afternoon in Willimantic, Connecticut, came from the parents and students when I told the parents they were within five years of knowing what they were talking about once again. Parents, and students, realize that the parent-child relationship changes with maturity to an adult-adult relationship and then, with age, to a child-parent arrangement where we need guidance from our children to meet the challenges of old age.

It is my opinion that there are three gifts which a parent can give a child that will greatly enhance the likelihood of success. These gifts are:

> *LOVE.* Active and enduring love, of God, of self, and of neighbor. If this sounds familiar, then you may be Jewish, Christian, Muslim, Buddhist, or Taoist. Love is the greatest gift, and according to Jesus, the Great Commandment.

> *STRUCTURE.* Great parents set high goals, grand expectations, and limits to acceptable behaviors. My greatest "problem children" at the university inevitably come from homes gone wild with freedom. Real freedom acknowledges its limits and boundaries. It implies responsibility. Students will forever want to know how far they can go, and how soon.

TAKING CHILDREN SERIOUSLY. This gift requires listening. We can practice "adultism" if we do not listen, which implies to the child, "I know better than you do because I am older." Age can bring wisdom, but this is not guaranteed. You reap what you sow with children. As I expect my children to listen to me, I should listen to them and take their thoughts seriously. Teachers who take students seriously are successful. Parents who listen early on may well find their children with open ears when life's lessons can be shared and taught.

The reality of parenthood is this:

The child you carried and loved today will be the caretaker who comforts you in old age tomorrow.

The relationship evolves, and part of parenting is letting go.

Giving the gifts of love, structure, and "taking seriously" will greatly enhance the chances for student success and good parent-child relationships. Someday...they will thank you!

The Psychology of Letting Go:

Loosening the Apron Strings

"If a little tree grows in the shade of a larger tree, it will die small."

Senegalese Proverb

I loved my mother when she was living, and I love her now even after her death. She gave me many gifts including:

My life

Love

A "Can't Never Did Anything" Attitude

For these things I will be eternally grateful to her. But she never let go...she held me tight, psychologically. She called me Bill or Billy until her death, decades after I had taken the original name she gave me, Will.

How tightly are you holding your child? I appreciate the fact that you want the best for your children. That is in your job description. But, do you know what your child wants? Are his dreams, her dreams known to you? The fact is, Father *didn't* always know best, and Ricky Nelson died a cocaine-related death in the midst of TV's perfect family.

Please do not go away, or worse, give up. But please...let go. The greater the fury caused by ear or nose piercing, the greater the chance another body part will follow. Children go through stages.

Let me ask you one question:

If your child studies the major chosen by you and ends up miserable, is that a good thing? Who wins?

Your child will have a "Declaration of Independence Day" someday. This I promise you! It can be a bloody revolution or a negotiated peace.

It is my guess that you can remember a time when you made an error in judgment or a serious mistake. Are you at a point in your life where you can allow your child the right to choose and experience the consequences of those choices? I hope so! Be careful not to cast such a big shadow that your offshoots cannot grow.

The Empty Nest:

Where Did Everyone Go?

"The best thing about the future is that it comes only one day at a time."

Abraham Lincoln

I am writing this chapter with a great sadness in my heart. I am writing now too with a great joy. The joy is that I have children, four of them. They are three girls and a boy. They are shining beams of light giving radiance to any day, even my darkest moments.

The sadness is that one day they will leave our home. I know this is natural. I know this is normal. I know that I wrote the last chapter on letting go. I also know that my nest will seem empty when I see them fly with wings like eagles to places I can't imagine or never dreamed of going.

What I am learning from my joy and sadness is that I had better stay in touch with my wife because, God willing, she will remain at our nest with me. If we become strangers when the children have gone, then we will have trouble adjusting to the quiet place left in place of activities.

I wish now to extend my sincere and heartfelt admiration and empathy for single parents, who by death or divorce have raised a family alone. Yours is the brightest star, your commitment the highest. Parenting pushes my wife and me to the limits of our patience and aptitude. How do you do it alone? You are amazing!

Single or coupled, one day the dust will settle, the crowd will exit, the house, apartment, or trailer will quiet. My hope is that we have lived each day with passion and appreciation of the fact that nothing lasts forever, save the grace of God.

I hope we are the sort of parents whose rearing renders our home a place of frequent visits and calls from our children. One day at a time!

The Big Transition:

From Child to Friend to...

"We should behave to our friends as we would wish our friends to behave to us."

Aristotle

There will come a time when you can remember what happened fifty years ago, but you cannot recall what you had for lunch this afternoon. How will you want to be treated?

When you find yourself baffled by the medications you are taking, what will you hope someone will say or do for you?

Today's child is tomorrow's parent. I am not talking about your grandchildren. I am talking about you! Invest your time, monies, and energies well today and reap the harvest of your good nature and goodwill tomorrow. Allow your child to grow into the man or woman he or she has the unique potential to be. The Chinese philosopher said, "If you love it, let it go. If it comes back to you, it was yours. If it doesn't, it never was." Trust your child to become a friend, independent and strong.

The Evolving Involving Parent:

Students Learn by Watching

"Between saying and doing many a pair of shoes is worn out."

Italian proverb

It is no secret that when a conflict exists between what you say and what you do, the observer will almost always believe what you do. "Action speaks louder than words" is one way to say it. "A picture is worth a thousand words" is another.

A parent who expects intellectual development and evolution from a child should role model the same. A parent who wants the child involved in school should be involved too. The young learn by watching. What do they see?

Not all examples are good, but the student can learn in either case. Show your child growth and development in your own person, stay involved, and watch your student model your example.

The crab instructs its young, "Walk straight ahead, like me." Set a good example for your children.

18

The Good Consumer:

Let the Buyer Beware

"A university should be a place of light, of liberty, and of learning."

Benjamin Disraeli

◦══◦

71

You are the consumer of the product education. I want you to be a good consumer, which means you understand that upon which you are spending your monies.

The university, like any responsible business, will put its best foot forward. Make sure you "test drive" the campus before you invest your down payment and, more importantly, your son or daughter.

When I purchased my Hot Springs hot tub, they sent me a list of happy customers in town. I called around and sought their advice. Should I do less on the campus that will educate my child's future?

You are becoming a shareholder at the college or university of your son or daughter's choice.

- Check the prospectus (catalog and promotional literature).

- Talk to other shareholders (parents and students).

- Meet the CEO (president) and her or his officers (administrators and faculty).

- Visit the job site or production facility (university campus).

If more parents and students took their consumerism more seriously, we would have fewer drop- or stop-outs, and students would finish their degrees sooner, and with less trouble caused by transfers or wasted time.

Make sure your student is not in the dark and is truly going to a place of higher learning.

The Questioner:

There are No Dumb Questions When You are Writing Checks

"No matter what accomplishments you make, somebody helps you."

Wilma Rudolf

I was meeting with the Mother's Club of a fraternity at Oregon State University. Twenty concerned and caring mothers had gathered for Mom's Weekend festivities. I asked each to introduce herself, tell me who her son or daughter was, and what year and major her child was in at OSU. To my amazement, five mothers could not tell me what year their sons were in school. "How will you know when to stop writing checks to the University?" I asked. It was very quiet in the room.

No question is foolish when you are paying the bill. Your child can tell you it's none of your business, but please, ask away! The university should be held accountable, as well. You are going to pay again if the college turns out a defective (*translation:* unemployable product; *translation:* your child). No one does anything alone. Do your part...ask good questions.

High Expectations:
On Raising the Bar

"Let our children grow tall and some taller than others if they have it in them to do so."

Margaret Thatcher

"**N**o one will ever break Babe Ruth's home run record." "It can't be done...a four-minute mile is impossible." "Lou Gehrig's consecutive game record is untouchable." "Americans will never drive small cars." "Women in the workplace? No way!" "Slaves as full people? Never gonna happen." "If man was meant to fly, God would have given him wings." "That will happen when the Berlin Wall comes down."

Hello...are you listening to yourself? What messages, what expectations are you giving to and setting for your children? My experience has taught me that with high hopes, encouragement, support, and expectations come high goals, noble objectives, and student success.

Your child can live up or down to your expectations. Set your sights high with your feet standing fully on the ground.

- Set incremental and achievable goals and expectations.
- Celebrate achievement.
- Enjoy successes.
- Set new goals.
- Repeat.

Say not, "if you graduate...," but rather "when you graduate...." Empower; do not enable. Encourage; do not discourage.

Then watch with pride as your child clears the bar. And should he fail, should she not make the height, be there to comfort, console, and challenge. But be there. Help him rise, dust her off, then step back as they try again. What you say is irrelevant compared to your presence. Through good times and bad, successes and failures, they will grow, with care, to their tallest places.

The Informed Parent:

Read the Catalog, the Contracts, the Books

"There is no such thing as making the miracle happen spontaneously and on the spot. You've got to work."

Martina Arroyo

I hope the theme of parental and guardian involvement is becoming exceedingly clear. The family is going to college; the student will be attending in person, but all of you are going.

READ THE CATALOG: In it you might discover that "hate speech" results in expulsion and criminal proceedings. Many students read this from their jail cells for the first time.

READ THE CONTRACTS: What will it cost you if your student decides to move out of the residence hall mid-term? To an apartment? To a fraternity or sorority? Is there a difference?

READ THE STUDENT'S TEXTBOOKS: You might learn something. The information in the world is doubling every three years, and besides, if you are reading the books, then you will know what your child is studying. It is clearly win/win. Give Clancy and Grisham a break and order some textbooks again from the bookstore.

You have to work to stay current and in tune with what the next generation is experiencing and thinking.

Today, that changes daily, if not hourly, on the Internet, MTV, and E-mail. Don't get left behind. Knowledge is power!

The Good Guardian, The Good Parent:

On Making Amends

"Govern a family as you would cook a small fish — very gently."

Chinese Proverb

There are two phrases that must become ever present in each guardian or parent's vocabular arsenal. They are:

I love you

and

I am sorry.

Sometimes things have not turned out exactly as you would have liked due to factors too numerous to consider. Please do not leave the campus without saying, "I love you," "I am sorry," or both. You have no guarantees in life that there will be another time to make amends. I believe that, as a theoretically more mature adult, it is the parent's or guardian's job to build bridges, mend fences, and make amends.

Please never go to sleep or drive off leaving an argument unhealed or at least undiscussed. Take time out, back off, but part knowing that your student knows he or she is loved. My students with the deepest problems wrestle with questions about their self-worth and loveability.

Be man or woman enough to say "I am sorry." It will not kill you and may repair a precious relationship. I do not expect you to be perfect, just honest with yourself and your child. Govern yourself and your loved ones gently.

The Self-Addressed
Stamped Envelope Please:

Keeping in Touch

"We can do no great things — only small things with great love."

Mother Theresa

Here is an idea for every parent who has wondered if his or her child will be all right at school and will keep in touch:

Give your student a self-addressed stamped envelope for each week of the current term. Twelve weeks = twelve self-addressed stamped envelopes.

At least the envelopes will communicate care and motivate your student to call or fax. If you get E-mail, your interaction can be fabulously easy. A "have a great day" posted on a midterm test morning could be a big mood elevator.

This is a small thing done with great love.

24

The Care Package:
A Little Piece of Heaven

"One of the oldest human needs is having someone to wonder where you are when you don't come home at night."

Margaret Mead

Here is another specific tip for parents, guardians, or families who want to say "We miss you" in more than words.

Mail a "care package" to the student during the week before finals each term. This is a stressful time that usually means late nights and a lot of pressure with preparation for final examinations.

Send cookies, candies, Lifesavers, gum, tea bags, and so forth, with a note. We do this at our church the Sunday before finals for our college attendees, and it is a big hit! Let them see that you are wondering how they are doing. They need to know it matters what they do!

The Home and Away Schedule:

The Balanced Schedule

"He who is being carried does not realize how far the town is."

Nigerian Proverb

"**V**isit often, son." "Come visit us, dear." Operative word: visit. I am hoping you will see your student often, but not too often. Here is my theory:

Every weekend spent at home is one less weekend for your child to get to know his or her roommate, campus activities, library, and new environment.

Piaget indicated that there is no growth without a readiness phase, caused usually by anxiety over a new environment or change. Balance the home and away schedule, as they do in sports. Please don't help your child avoid growth at all costs. He or she can carry the weight of reasonable change.

The Dirty Laundry:
Stop Doing It

"The sun will set without your assistance."

Yiddish Proverb

Your home is not a dumping station for recreational vehicles or your child's laundry. Pack some Tide and Downy in their bags, introduce them to the wash cycle, and let them grow up.

Stop Doing Their Laundry (while they are at school).

If you have some Zen need to wash their clothes during breaks and vacations, that is your decision. But allowing weekly dumping of dirty underwear at your house does not teach responsibility; it encourages dependence. The clothes will get washed without your assistance. Someday you won't be there to enable their dependence. Set them free...start the wash cycle!

PART III
STUDENT SECTION

The First-Year Student:

Making the Transition to College

"Nothing pains some people more than having to think."

Martin Luther King, Jr.

Even with all the exciting and meaningful work coming out of the Freshman Year Experience at the University of South Carolina, and even though colleges and universities have renewed interest in and have committed themselves to freshman and new student orientation, one fact remains:

Half the students who start do not persist and graduate. They do not make it.

Why? Why don't more first-year students stay and graduate? Clearly, the transition is a tough one, but with insight and effort, the path from start to finish can be smoothed, illuminated, and completed.

Most students whom I have observed having difficulty have been bright enough to succeed but had other shortcomings that negatively impacted their initial experience.

COMMON PROBLEMS:

- Student takes the entire summer off to "do Europe" and loses the competitive edge over a "few" beers in Munich.

- While campuses often propose summer readings, students do not do them and begin behind. I was asked to read *Coming of Age in Mississippi* and *This Boy's Life* at one school because I was the Freshman Orientation speaker. I read them and was moved by them. When I asked the audience of 1,000 freshmen who had read the books, approximately 200 had taken the time. It was a lost opportunity to start strong, informed, and prepared.

- The student embraces a full-blown participation in campus social life and forgets to address the curricular requirements of a college education.

- Freshmen and new students think that the first year is just to "get the kinks out," or "get your feet on the ground," failing to see that the first-year grades are averaged with the last year's efforts.

- Inflated grades in high school render the student unaware of what become glaring academic as well as personal deficiencies.

SOME IDEAS:

- Read the suggested reading early in the summer.

- Take some time off, but don't get totally out of some routine. You are training for an important phase of your life.

- Solicit addresses of juniors and seniors in honor societies and ask for campus-specific tips for success in the first year.

- Participate in any Summer Orientation offerings given by the college or university.

- If you have any idea what you will be studying, get a fall term reading list and get going.

- If room assignments are made early, contact your room-mate and plan for a calm and peaceful move-in. Who will bring what?

- Get to campus as soon as they will let you begin.

- Buy your books early. It is not uncommon to have some classes sell out their books and some late buyers waiting three weeks for the text (and falling behind).

- Take a tour of the campus research centers with a library professional and find out what computer-assisted learning facilities are on campus or near it.

- Check the technological capacities of the place where you will live. Can the hall or apartment handle your computer and sound system?

- Set a regular exercise program in the campus recreation center. It eases stress.

REMEMBER THIS:

When it comes to being new, no one is an expert. Ask the question that seems dumb, because 100 other people will be wondering the same thing. If you are a growing person in life, then you are always a freshman at something. Winners are not afraid to fail. They just see failure as a temporary glitch on the way to success. Be different! Stand out! Succeed! Use your head and *think*!

The Commuter Student:

Tips for Time Management

"You can't 'have it all' — nature doesn't work that way, and finally there are only so many hours in the day. It is, however, almost always possible to have more; having less often means producing less."

Mary Catherine Bateson

If you are returning to school or your child is commuting, then life on campus will be quite different from the residential experience. This does not mean you cannot have a quality college experience. It does mean you must utilize and manage your time efficiently.

SOME SUGGESTIONS:

- Locate early the commuter parking spaces nearest your first or last class. Time is short, there are traffic delays, and it is good to plan in advance.

- Can you receive credit for job experience or life experience? Most commuter students I have known have been holding one or two jobs as well as going to school. Can one of these jobs fit into an internship? Internships often turn into full-time jobs after graduation.

- Ask about the commuter lounges and/or lockers on campus. Is there a place to study between classes, make phone calls, check on job or family goings-on?

- Is there a campus center for day care? Often these centers are staffed by child development majors getting practicum credit, and the programs are quite educational.

- Check with Student Activities for a list of activities during the day or evening while you are on campus.

You can enrich your college experience with programs that fit your schedule.

- Create a program, if it does not exist, whereby you can be a social member of a residence hall. Some campuses have experimented with this idea to create on-campus involvement for commuters.

- If your child is living at home, make sure to talk about the new relationship. Someone going to college probably has a right to be treated differently than a high school senior. Respect is the key, and it needs to be mutual.

- Ask your professors if you can tape the lectures for the purpose of listening to them during your commute. Even if you get stuck in traffic you can be making progress toward a degree.

Commuting to and from the college or university can be a dreadful experience or a rewarding one. Living at home can save money if all parties are committed to and involved in the process of achieving a higher education. Maximize your time, turn your drive and work into advantages, and get involved in co-curricular programs and activities.

The Transfer Student:

Staking a New Claim

"Life is either a great adventure, or it is nothing."

Helen Keller

Dr. Nancy Schlossberg once conducted research at the University of Maryland and discovered that students who felt as if they belonged, or "mattered," tended to persist and graduate, while those who felt alienated or "marginalized" did not persist and graduate at the level of the "belongers."

It is imperative if your student is transferring to encourage him or her to get involved immediately and "stake a new claim." Be sure that the maximum number of credit hours has been accepted. Do not give up. Do not lose credit hours on the whim of an advisor. Any credible campus will have an orientation for transfers. Attend it. It would be my opinion that when your child begins to transfer for the second or third time, there may be other issues at work. Perhaps it is time to encourage a break from school to gain some life experience. Nothing makes school seem better than a minimum-wage job.

Make life count by making a higher education work. Sometimes one must transfer to do this. Be careful not to transfer with the thought that all problems will go away. Transfer to a better place to achieve an education that fits your long-term goal. Be adventuresome, be daring, but most importantly, finish what you started!

The New Student Orientation:

A Good Map for the Journey

"J can honestly say that J was never affected by the question of success of an undertaking. Jf J felt it was the right thing to do, J was for it, regardless of the possible outcome."

Golda Meir

E very responsible campus provides an orientation program much as a corporation provides training and education for new workers. Week of Welcome. WOW!

Summer Orientation - Advising Program SOAP

The O(rientation) Team

Orientation provides an opportunity to meet other students, faculty, and staff. Every effort should be made to attend a session before the year begins. Students will be involved in the orientation program, and this is great. They tend to be bright, successful, and great resources of information about the campus. But the entire program should not consist of them. If there are not a good number of faculty and staff involved, ask "why not?"

When you leave campus, have a good idea of:

- Test dates for majors and basic courses

- Tuition and its payment plans

- How safe the campus is

- What the registration-for-classes process will be like

- What the university promises to deliver for your tuition

- How long the average student takes to graduate

- The name of a contact person in case of an emergency

Getting a college education is clearly the right thing to do. A quality orientation to the university experience will get you on the right course. If the campus cannot plan, organize, and run a good orientation experience, then what could make you believe the rest of the experience will suddenly become meaningful and professional?

The Early Warning Signs:

Distance, Ignorance, and Silence

"Unhappy people place too many demands on themselves. They insist that they do everything perfectly. They allow no mistakes in their life."

Billy Mills

"We haven't heard from you." "I know...I've been busy." "How have you been?" "Fine." "How's school going?" "OK." "How are you doing in your classes?" "Good." "Will you give us a call this weekend?" "Sure." "Love you." "Bye."

When, and I hope you do not, you get this call, it should worry you. If your student is:

- Distant in his/her statements

- Ignorant about specific class progress

- Silent when asked questions

...then you should go visit, have them come home, or contact a resident assistant, dean, or faculty member to make contact.

I would rather have you accused of caring too much than of benign neglect. It strikes me that students should be able to provide some direct insight into their life on campus if they are attending class, studying, and getting involved in co-curricular activities.

THINK ABOUT:

- Asking open-ended questions: "Of all your classes, which one do you like the best? Why?" or "Tell me about your favorite professor."

- Telling your child you love him or her and that you want to be kept up on what's happening

- Asking your student to bring some friends home for a weekend or holiday

Billy Mills is right...everything in life is not going to go perfectly. Expecting so results in frustration and unhappiness. But when you feel distance and silence creeping into your relationship with your student, trust your feelings and experience and get involved. Initiate the call and break the silence.

The Children of Divorce:

A Whole Lot of Company

"And yet the central survival skill is surely the capacity to pay attention and respond to changing circumstances, to learn and adapt, to fit into new environments beyond the safety of the temple precincts."

Mary Catherine Bateson

When I left for college, it was a beautiful sunny day in Southern California. There are only two seasons in Los Angeles: nice, and nicer. This was nicer...late summer, and the family was gathered at 132 N.W. Grandview Avenue, Covina, California, to say good-bye.

Our family is an interesting collection. Isn't yours? Both my parents are deceased, but I can see them on the parkway in 1971 as clearly as if it were yesterday.

Bettye Jean Tobin had come west from Sac City, Iowa, on the back of a motorcycle to escape life in a midwestern town. Her boyfriend died in a horrible crash with his motorcycle, my mother as passenger, sliding underneath an 18 wheeler on Signal Avenue in Long Beach.

Jack R. Wilhelm had come to California for work after watching his father's farm in Rocky Ford, Colorado, be repossessed after his father passed away. Jimmy, his dad, died when he was twelve, and I believe Jack never recovered from the sadness.

Jack was my stepfather, though he remains Dad because my real father died when Bettye was pregnant with me. Sometimes when I hear my students talk about what a son-of-a-bitch their fathers are, it occurs to me, "I wish I had had the time to reach that conclusion about my own father."

Jack and Bettye married before World War II, cheated on each other, and divorced. My mother married Will S. Keim, Jr., after the failure of his first marriage, and they tried for eight years to get pregnant.

Mission accomplished, my blood father died of complications following surgery.

After Jack returned from the war to end all wars, Bettye and he were married, Round II. Therefore, I am left with the inescapable conclusions:

1. Had my blood father not been divorced from his first wife, I would not have been conceived.

2. If Jack and Bettye had not been divorced, then I would not have been born as the result of Will, Jr., and Bettye "The Only" getting together.

3. Life is really strange.

We live in a time now when divorce is once again being stigmatized as "the wrong option." Certainly our divorce rate is too high, but equally true is the reality that some people were not born to be together.

I thought for many years that I was weird, that I was the only Little Leaguer, high school student, college athlete, doctoral candidate, etc., from a divorced home.

Wake up! We are many, maybe even the majority. We are the children of divorce. The ability to cope with change has been forced upon us. We can adapt to changing circumstances. Conversely, we will forever put an asterisk by the word TRUST. When our lovers say, "I will always be with you. I'll always love you," we know from our parents' experience and example that love does not always last forever.

Do not feel guilty! This is not the point. Be aware; know that we are fine, tested by real life experience. We will survive. And know that you're amongst great company in this understanding.

It is possible your child has not forgiven you yet for divorcing his or her other parent. Or perhaps your "ex" is all the blame. Time will ease the pain if one thing occurs:

Your child knows, without reservation, that he or she is loved!

(God willing, by all responsible adults concerned.)

"The central survival skill...," writes Bateson, "is surely the capacity to pay attention and respond to changing circumstances." Children of divorce are:

In good company, and prepared to deal with change.

This is the upside of divorce. This is how life is.

The Expert Theory:
100 Miles from Home

"A cynical young person is almost the saddest sight to see because it means that he or she has gone from knowing nothing to believing in nothing."

Maya Angelou

Did you know that the national drop-out rate for the freshman year hovers around 50 percent? After the first year, half the students have transferred, stopped attending, taken a job, or sought another activity rather than school. Why is this?

Did they choose the wrong university?

Were they overwhelmed by intense study?

Did they have unrealistic goals for college?

Or, were they underwhelmed by their experience and consumed by cynicism that they learned from the characters and situations on campus?

This is a tough thing to say, but I believe it with my entire being: Teachers have a responsibility to be informed, honest, caring, skilled in sharing information, and hopeful.

Many students develop a rabid cynicism based on hypercritical professors who believe, or at least propose, that our country is the root of all evil and we are all going to hell in a handbasket. Their "mid-life crisis" analysis stalls the young mind and facilitates a "what difference does it make" philosophy that crashes down into:

What difference do I make?

This was not my personal experience because I went to a small, private school committed to philosophy and in tenuring practices to good teaching. I knew my professors who were all Ph.D. caliber or terminally degreed, i.e., Rabbi Rosenberg for Old Testament classes.

Does your child know his or her instructors? Do students ever really see the professors who wrote the books the university is so proud of?

A university education is about knowledge, truth, skills, growth, and hope. Your student, properly challenged and inspired, should be excited as never before about campus academics and life. If not, find out why. Get involved. Your student should return during and after the first year like "an expert," fired up about what she knows, "one hundred miles" from campus and yet light years from his high school self.

If, as Dr. Angelou asserted in her opening quote, your student "has gone from knowing nothing to believing in nothing," then the university has failed him or her. Be on guard! Be a good consumer. Find a campus environment that empowers students to learn to love to learn. One that creates a hopeful world and national view. A place that educates and puts forth change agents who love themselves and want to make a difference. A place where "experts," hopeful experts, are formed!

34

The Cycle of Life:

Child, Friend, and Parent

"Eternity is not something that begins after you are dead. It is going on all the time. We are in it now."

Charlotte Perkins Gilman

During a wedding one August day, I observed a video slide presentation of Scott Thiebert and Jennifer Winquist. They were shown as infants, young toddlers, bright-eyed children, teenagers, then young adults. The emotive effect on the congregation was deep and real. People were touched, and though my job as officiating minister called me to stay cool and calm, I was misty-eyed watching these two bright and beautiful people age before my eyes on video, and all in four minutes.

As I look at my own children, I believe time goes just as fast in real life. Born today, ten years old tomorrow. Sunrise, sunset, but warp speed times ten to the seventh power. Everyone who is a parent knows this. The question is:

> What are we doing about it? How is this knowledge impacting our behavior? Our relationship with our children?

Here is how I see it. You have children, raise them to adulthood, and then at some point, the child-turned-adult becomes parental, lending advice and a hand as we grow into older age. We should all ask ourselves:

> Am I treating my child the way I will want her or him to treat me later?

> If I will reap what I sow, then what seeds am I spreading into the life of the one who will see me from fall to winter?

Gilman advises us that "eternity is going on now." And how right she is! As you read this book, will you begin to see each day (and remind me to do the same) as an investment in a life well lived? Can we step back from minute and tiny disappointments and see the big picture? As we carry our children in our arms and then off to college, let us know we did our very best at creating hopeful, loving children who saw life's possibilities, through our eyes, as good.

They will one day give back to us what we have given to them. Our eternity is right before our eyes. Let us see this clearly!

The Returning Student:

This Is Where You Belong

"He who would leap high must take a long run."

Danish Proverb

When you think of a typical college student, what images do you get? It was common twenty years ago to have a relatively homogenous group of students in terms of age, values, and experiences. Things have changed!

If you are returning to school or have a student who is "starting again," then recognize that there will be a lot of folks just like you! You do belong in school, and the only person you need to convince is yourself.

Enlightened faculty, staff, and students will welcome your real-life experience. Do not be afraid to share it. Please be aware that many colleges will now give credit for life experiences. Check this out before enrolling. What you have done matters and may be credited by selected departments on campus.

The road is long to some places, but that doesn't stop us from going there if we really want to see what's at the other end of our journey. "You must take a long run to jump high," the Danes advise. If your run is long, then perhaps a great jump is ahead. My guess is that the university will help you set the bar higher than you ever thought you could go!

The Diversity Dimension:

Affirming the Difference

"Injustice anywhere is a threat to justice everywhere."

Martin Luther King, Jr.

Somehow the discussion of diversity has detoured away from its centrality to the American experience and into its negative impact on campus and society. Seemingly educated men and women debate the differences between us rather than celebrating our common human spirit. The time has come for us to seek "common ground," a place where all cultures can shine and share with each other. A place where the operative word in African American, Euro American, Asian American, Hispanic American, Native American, et al. is *American*. None of us need give up our heritage to forge ahead in the creation of genuine human community. I wish I could tell you this is the current environment on today's college and university campuses. Your student will likely find her- or himself in a politically charged, nearly hostile environment of political correctness and conservative backlash. Your child, despite free speech guarantees in the Constitution and Bill of Rights, may be told what he or she can and cannot say. Groups of all colors, ages, and orientations force the issue with a true lack of civility, care, and love of neighbor.

There clearly is, at least in all state and federally supported campuses and ethically in all university sites, no room for prejudice based on race, creed, color, national origin, sexual orientation, or age. Most of these are protected by law and Constitution; all are covered in standards of ethical conduct set forth in every major world religion and philosophy.

Your student, and you, must understand, as Dr. King so clearly said, that "injustice anywhere is a threat to justice everywhere." We all have a proposed right to life, liberty, and the pursuit of happiness.

I hope you will encourage your student by example to:

1. Tolerate Diversity, then...

2. Understand Diversity, then...

3. Affirm Diversity.

America is a "nation of mutts," a series of various tribes, peoples, immigrants, and refugees, those seeking asylum and a better way of life. Diversity is our greatest national strength, not a weakness. Encourage your child to make friends with others. Teach her or him not to judge based on superficial characteristics. Black and white, rich and poor, brown, yellow, dark and pale, old and young, male and female, believer and non-believer, gay and straight, our foremothers and -fathers have created a national mosaic where we can all make a contribution and a difference. Teach your children to honor the diversity that has made America great.

There are two things we have in common above all else: the ability to love and the need to be loved. Teach by example the lessons of love, and watch your child flourish and grow!

The Intercollegiate Student Athlete:

Pulling on the P.A.D.S.

"Ability may get you to the top, but it takes character to keep you there....Success is peace of mind knowing you did your best."

John Wooden, Teacher and Coach, UCLA Basketball
Retired, 10 National Championships

I played four years of varsity baseball at a small Division I school. I immediately discovered two fundamental differences between this and high school athletics:

1. The players were a lot better.
2. Balancing practice and games with academics and social life was challenging at best.

If your child is at a high-powered Division I college or university in a revenue-generated sport, the pressure will be immense. Coaches, despite university and NCAA encouragements and publicity to the contrary, are paid to win. Rare is the character-builder, the teacher, the coach who keeps his or her job without winning. Division I AA, II, III, and NAIA participation lessens the pressure, but the tightrope walk between court and class is difficult to walk.

Please share these four ideas with your student athlete:

1. *PASSION.* Encourage your child to play as long as she or he is in love, passionately, with the sport.

2. *ACADEMICS.* Teach your student athlete that she or he will in all probability (97 to 99 percent) earn a living through her or his knowledge, not athletic ability. The first priority is to go to class, study, and *graduate.* Remind your student that the key word in athletic scholarship is *scholar.* A coach who says differently is a liar and a detriment to your child's well-being.

3. *DRUGS.* These have no place in athletics. Drug use will either render the athlete incompetent or ineligible. Pay particular attention to rapid muscle gain, nearly unbelievable strength gains, irritability, hair loss, acne, and violent outbursts. These may be clear signs of steroid use, which is illegal and punishable by suspension and revocation of scholarship.

4. *SEX.* Student athletes are fit, bright, active, and popular, and opportunities for sexual activity will follow. Teach your student athlete that one out of every 250 college students is HIV positive. Sexually transmitted diseases are at a fifty-year high. Sexual responsibility and abstention may well enhance performance and your child's ability to stay well and ultimately alive.

Attend as many games as you can, let the student athlete know that you are aware of pressure, and know your child may well learn as much on the field as off!

The Greek Student:

Five Questions You Must Ask

"Fraternities and sororities should graduate better men and women, with higher grades, more school spirit, a sense of community responsibility, and an understanding of leadership, than if the students did not join. If they do, I am for them, if they do not, then they are a concern on the college landscape."

Will Keim, Ph.D.

My fraternity is proud of 162 years of history formed on justice, character, appreciation of culture, and friendship. We celebrate the non-secrecy pledge whereby we have no secret ritual, handshakes, or initiations. We were the first fraternity that opened its doors widely to diverse members. Our alumni who have changed the world include Dr. Linus Pauling, double Nobel Laureate, Dr. Karl Menninger, James McDonnell, James Garfield, Lester Pearson, Lou Holtz, Michael Eisner, Herb Brownell, Charles Evans Hughes, and Peter Ueberroth.

At the same time, we struggle, as do all fraternities and sororities, with accusations and realities, including alcohol and drug abuse, racism, sexism, hazing, and poor scholarship.

I would encourage you to encourage your student to go through rush, the membership recruitment phase of Greek life, and ask five central questions:

1. *WILL I BE HAZED?* The answer should be "No!" Hazing is illegal in thirty-seven states and clearly against every single fraternity and sorority national and international policy. It has no place in the Greek system and has caused sixty deaths in the last fifteen years. Any answer short of "No!," such as, "It depends on what you mean by hazing," or "Do you mean physical hazing or psychological hazing?" simply means hazing is occurring and could endanger your son or daughter. "No!" is the answer you want to hear.

2. *IS THERE A DRUG PROBLEM IN THE CHAPTER?* Be clear that drug use has been up on college campuses for ten consecutive years. Primarily this means in marijuana use, which is perilous given the 1990 Drug Free Campus and Community Act that basically doubles the penalty upon conviction. The answer should be, "No! Our Chapter does not tolerate alcohol abuse or drug use."

3. *WILL I BE FORCED TO DRINK ALCOHOL?* Alcohol is not only our national drug of choice, but it is readily accessible on the college campus. Alcohol is not the problem. Abuse of alcohol is the problem. Abuse is hard to corral because it can result from chemical heredity, social upbringing, peer pressure, or a host of other factors. Pledging, or joining, a fraternity should be alcohol free as directed by university and fraternal policy.

Ask your student directly about the pledging process. Any hesitation or evasive equivocation on the pledge's part should alert you to a problem. Alcohol and pledging are a very dangerous combination.

4. *WHAT IS THIS CHAPTER'S ACADEMIC RANKING ON CAMPUS?* Answer A: "Out of _____ Chapters on campus our ranking is _____."

This is an honest response. Even if a Chapter is ranked low and states a commitment to improve, then this is an honest group of men or women.

Answers B and C: "We don't keep that kind of information." *Translation:* "We don't talk about this because it is not a big selling point." Or, "Grades are not that important to us." In either translation, this is not a group that understands the outcome of mediocrity on future success.

5. *WILL MY DATE BE RESPECTED WHEN HE OR SHE COMES TO THE CHAPTER?* If I told you that groups of men who called themselves gentlemen get in fights with fists over women, would you believe me?

If I told you women who call themselves sisters date each other's boyfriends, would you think I was lying?

Men and women in fraternities and sororities will tell you they are scholars, leaders, brothers, sisters, community servants, and socially responsible people. All I am asking you to do is to hold the Greeks accountable for "walking their talk," that is, practicing what they preach. And that includes treating dates, boyfriends and girlfriends, parents, and siblings with respect.

The differences between a good Greek Chapter and a bad one are like night and day. Open your eyes and look around. Your student's future, and life, might depend upon your vigilance.

The Major Decision:
Choosing a Pathway

"Choose a job you love, and you will never have to work a day in your life."

Confucius

∽⌇∿

R eports indicate that the typical college and university student changes her or his major 3.4 times during the college career. There are some students who come in pre-law and then practice it as attorneys. Some unique individuals know their direction early and stick to it. Most students wander from their initial choice to a major they never dreamed of or knew anything about.

Be aware that a significant number of employers will tell you that they will teach your student what they need to know after employment. One Australian CEO told me frankly, "I don't care what their majors are, mate. I'll retrain them anyway. I am looking for people with good attitudes and good communication skills."

Forcing your children into majors or career choices they despise or dislike will result in unhappy and unfulfilled young professionals. They may make money, but without a job they enjoy, their professional life will be miserable.

My advice is this:

> Find something you love to do,
> and learn to do it well enough that
> someone will pay you to do it.

Life is short and your student has a right, and need, to reinvent the wheel, make his or her own mistakes, and experience life firsthand. You had your turn; now is their turn to carry the burning torch.

The Ethical Student:

A Four-Step Model to Better Decision Making

"J hope J shall always possess firmness and virtue enough to maintain what J consider the most enviable of all titles, the character of an honest man."

George Washington

There are four questions that you and your student could ask that would render much better decision making. Do you want to know what they are? Good!

BEFORE YOU ACT

1. *What is my intention?* Why am I doing this?_____

_____

2. *What is the law or applicable policy* relevant to my action?_____

3. *What are the consequences of this action?*_____

_____

4. *What are my moral principles* regarding this action?

_____

We often tell ourselves and our children to stop and think. Now you can provide them with a four-step model to utilize when facing different choices and actions.

Or...you might encourage them to use the Grandma Test:

"Would you do this in front of your Grandma?"

If not, maybe this particular action can wait.

The Homesick Student:
Staying the Course

*"He that conceals his grief finds no
remedy for it."*

Turkish Proverb

O ne of the best-kept secrets of collegiate life and certainly one of the least-discussed experiences is that of homesickness. Almost everyone experiences it, some coping with a sense of loss and some actually leaving school for the friendlier confines of home.

If I ran a university, there would be open "homesick forums" where students could discuss their feelings, meet others experiencing their own version of the malaise, and find words and persons of encouragement. Sadly, these sessions are rare...as if talking about homesickness will increase its scope and size on campus.

What is happening is a grieving, a parting process of separation and loss similar to Elizabeth Kubler Ross' *Five Stages of Grieving*. I will present the stages with a Parent's and Student's translation of them. You may find yourself having similar feelings; be assured what you are going through is normal.

STAGES OF GRIEVING

Stage One: SHOCK AND DENIAL

    Parent: "I can't believe s/he is in college. Why, just yesterday

    _____."

    Student: "My God, this place is huge. I don't know anybody."

Stage Two: RAGE AND ANGER

    Parent: "Did he or she fall off the map? I'd appreciate a call now
        and then. How can he or she be so insensitive?"

Student: "Could they make it any harder to figure things out? My high school ran better than this!"

Stage Three: BARGAINING

Parent: "If I can just get through this term, then I'll be O.K. Come on, buck up. You're stronger than this."

Student: "I'll give this two more weeks. If it doesn't come around, I'm out of here."

Stage Four: DEPRESSION

Parent: "I should have spent more time with him/her when s/he was little. Where did the time go...It's so quiet here I can't stand it."

Student: "I've never been so lonely. No one laughs at my jokes. Maybe I picked the wrong school. I could transfer someplace closer to home."

Stage Five: ACCEPTANCE

Parent: "I'm going to be all right. S/he is doing what s/he needs to be doing and I'm so proud.

Student: "This place grows on you. I can't believe all the things going on. I'm hanging here this weekend for a movie and dance. I'm making it."

Shock and denial. Rage and anger. Bargaining. Depression. Acceptance. These are the five stages of grieving and homesickness. It is a grieving process of letting go and taking up. Letting go of the past and taking up a new direction in life.

THREE THINGS FOR PARENTS AND STUDENTS TO DO
TO COPE WITH HOMESICKNESS

Parent:

1. Talk to parents who have had children go to college. Perhaps your own parents or members of a Mom's or Dad's Club from your child's college. There is strength in numbers.
2. Talk to a counseling professional in your community. It is nice to receive adult confirmation regarding the normalcy of your feelings.
3. Call your student.

Student:

1. Share your feelings with your roommate. There is a real good chance s/he is experiencing the same feelings.
2. Discuss your feelings with your resident assistant, counselor, academic advisor, dean, or coach. These men and women are trained professionals who will lend you an ear and advice.
3. Call your parent.

There is no better medicine than the knowledge that you are valued and missed. As the Turkish proverb states, concealing grief brings no remedy for it. Get it off your chest, and you will begin the process of successfully coping with the university's little secret called homesickness.

The Personal Finance Plan:

Everything Has a Price Tag

"You can have nearly anything you can dream of...the reality though is that everything has a price tag. Are you willing to pay it?"

Will Keim

I fear this chapter will fall on deaf ears. It is a lesson poorly taught at the university. I could have titled the chapter:

Be Careful What You Wish for Because You Might Get It

Some examples:

"I want to be a doctor" means four years of undergraduate school, medical school, internship, and residency, for a total of ten to fifteen years of school, times tuition. Did I mention a personal life? Cost? $100,000? $200,000? Great job, big price tag.

"I'm thinking law." Translation: Join the ranks of 750,000 U.S. lawyers. You better be near the top of the class and know someone who can arrange a great clerkship. Great job, big price tag.

"I'm really not into school. I'm just here because I don't know what else to do." My version: No planning; average grades; limited vision; few prospects; moving home. It defies explanation why a young person would go to a place she or he does not like, refuse to go to class or study, practice boredom in its fullest debilitating power, and then pay money for the privilege.

"Everything has a price tag." Help your student figure out her goals; help him learn to dream; give her guidance and support; then assist him or her in fixing a psychological, physical, spiritual, and financial price tag on their aspiration. This will greatly encourage them to take college seriously as a place to prepare for life.

The Sexual Revolution:
Bad Moves and Body Bags

"If you make a mistake with sex in the '90s, there is a chance they'll carry you off campus in a body bag. It is called AIDS and nobody with the disease is laughing or bragging about their sexual prowess."

Will Keim

Simply put, it is a whole new ball game with the "sexual revolution." In fact, the only revolution I see is the revolting reality that students and parents do not seem to understand the severity of bad moves and bad choices with sex.

Consider:

One out of 100 college men in America is HIV positive.

Says who? Just a little place in Atlanta called the Center for Disease Control. Their research is based on tested blood samples given during all-campus blood drives. Sexually transmitted diseases (STDs) are at a fifty-year high. Anyone fooling around now and doing it unsafely and unprotected is a moron.

You may not like the idea of your student being sexual, but consider this:

My Question: How do you like the idea of them being dead? of suffering unimaginable disease and sickness? Are you prepared to watch the degradation of death by AIDS or not to be a grandparent because you failed to talk about sex, protection, and STDs?

Your Answer:

_____

_____

_____

If you believe in sexual abstinence until marriage, then teach that lesson with integrity, care, and forthrightness. You cannot scare them into submission; you must educate them into safe and sane behavior. I can make a strong case for abstinence...can you?

I would love for your student and you to read all my books and become friends. Or I can conduct your child's funeral. This choice is ours to make as parents and educators. Here is my theory:

> The more information we share, the more we care, the more open we are about human sexuality and the places it should and should not occur, the greater the chances that your child and my student will be alive to make you a grandparent and me a successful teacher.

The twenty-first century sexual revolution must be one of responsibility and informed choices. Anything less has catastrophic possibilities from which no one will benefit. Choose the light of education, not the darkness of ignorance.

44

Alcohol and You:
On the Rocks

"One of these days is none of these days."

English Proverb

f you were to ask the typical college student, How many of your friends drink? or, How many students on campus drink? most likely the response would be:

Everyone.

But consider this:

- Twenty percent of the entering freshman class does not drink at all.

- Thirty-five percent drink between one and five drinks per week.

What this means is that over 50 percent of the students drink responsibly.

Does your student? Do you?

It has been my experience that most student problems such as:

Poor scholarship	Fighting
Sexual misconduct	Date rape
Disciplinary actions	Racial incidents

...are alcohol-related at least three-fourths of the time. There are even some men's fraternities that have banned alcohol in the Chapter house. Did you know all sororities forbid alcohol in their Chapter houses?

"One of these days is none of these days," and the day is now for colleges and universities to put forth a coherent, developmental, and realistic policy on alcohol. The university's dirty little secret is that it tolerates alcohol abuse by students and faculty alike. This is not easy to say nor to hear. But the fact is this: The college and university enables alcohol use that is neither social nor responsible. As a parent you should discover the campus' view of alcohol and the steps it will take to teach low- or no-risk drinking.

Of course, this teaching should begin at home. But it should continue on campus with a "no-tolerance" policy for alcohol abuse and its horrible children: fighting, damage, racism, rape, poor scholarship, and death.

Your child's life may depend on the campus' willingness to intervene in abusive situations. Today, not tomorrow, is the day!

The Drug War:

The 1990 Drug-Free Campus and Community Act

"Don't give me any honey and spare me the sting."

Yiddish Proverb

I grew up at a time when drug use, in my case marijuana, was far from looked-down upon, and was about as societally acceptable in Southern California as drinking. Had I been caught, the penalty would have been a one-hundred-dollar fine and a nonrecorded misdemeanor charge.

Things have changed, yet students still recite the same old song. "Marijuana is just the same as alcohol. Maybe better because you don't have a hangover." We said it; they say it. But things have changed. My "potential misdemeanor" is now a "potential felony." How?

In a well-meaning effort to curb drug use on or near elementary, junior high, and high schools, and college and university campuses, the Congress has authorized legislation that can, at the judge's discretion, double the penalty for drug convictions where the use occurred within a mile of the aforementioned campuses. Try to find a place to get high a mile away from a school.

The result of possession and use of a very small amount of marijuana or other drug can be immense. Better put:

The Stakes of Student Mistakes Just Went Up.

Please be informed and please consider not starting usage or cutting down your current use. Teach your students by example, not rhetoric. Given a choice between what you say and what you do, they will almost always choose to "hear" what you do. The sting of drug use, if one is caught, is severe.

PART IV

CONCLUDING THOUGHTS

The Carrot, The Stick, and The Caress:

Thoughts on Inspiring Your Student

"The best horse needs a whip and the smartest person needs advice."

Yiddish Proverb

No one knows your student, your child, as well as you do. You should trust your experience. What motivates him or her to do his or her very best?

- *Carrot?* A promise ahead of things to come?

- *Stick?* A gentle nudge from behind?

- *Caress?* The power of human love?

No matter how self-sufficient your student appears, she or he still needs your:

Love

Concern

Advice

Give all three in abundance, and in the case of advice, pick your issues and know that timing is essential in lending your opinion to the discussion.

Students who watch parents wrestle, change, and grow will likely do the same. Lead, and inspire, by example.

The Maturing Student:
Taking a Person Seriously

"The God who gave us life, gave us liberty at the same time."

Thomas Jefferson

161

One of the greatest gifts a parent can give a maturing student is the gift of taking him or her seriously. Attempting to maintain a strict parent-child relationship with someone trying desperately to enter adulthood is a relationship-damaging posture. Phrases such as:

You've got to be kidding!

What are they teaching you at college?

You'll feel differently when you're my age.

I tried that...you'll see....

only cause distance. You certainly do not have to, nor should you agree with everything that is said, but take some time to consider the merit of what is being said and, most importantly, take your child seriously as a human being.

As you have given your child life, you must now allow for his or her liberty. Someday you will be gone. What will happen then if you have continued to make all the tough decisions? How will your child be able to cope, to choose, to direct him- or herself?

Take your maturing student and her or his problems seriously. Watch him or her grow into adulthood with love and an understanding of what it means to be a functioning adult. This is your gift to your child. Give it freely.

About the Author

D r. Will Keim has lectured to two million students on eight hundred campuses. His *Education of Character* lecture series is the most popular educational program on American college and university campuses.

He has been selected as the Outstanding Professor at Oregon State University; the Durwood Owen Recipient for Outstanding Interfraternalism; an Outstanding Man of America by the U.S. Jaycees; and holds numerous awards for excellence in leadership in higher education. Dr. Keim also was selected the 1996 Paul Harris Fellow by Rotary International in appreciation of "tangible and significant assistance given for the furtherance of better understanding and friendly relations among peoples of the world."

Dr. Keim's books and videos are staples of freshman orientation, resident assistant training, student athlete life-skills programs, and student leadership training. His corporate clients include AT&T, IBM, Delta Air Lines, Rotary International, and State Farm Insurance.

He is married, the father of four, and the campus minister at Oregon State for the Christian Church (Disciples of Christ).

49

The Graduate:
A Permit to Hunt

"The world cares very little about what a man or woman knows; it is what the man or woman is able to do that counts."

Booker T. Washington

Lynn D. W. Lukow, President of Jossey Bass Publishers, presents an interesting analysis of the worth of a college degree. He calls it "a permit to hunt" in places the non-degree-holder is not permitted to go. It is a license, not carte blanche, to begin, to commence the journey.

Business and society will not be impressed with the fact that your student took B.A. 311. All the "book learnin'" in the world pales in comparison to what a student can do. Look for colleges and universities that offer internships and externships. Chances for learning out of the classroom as well as in the classroom.

And guide your student toward fields of inquiry and study that interest him or her. You made your choices...are you happy? Let your student pick his or her own path. Help her or him understand the value of "a permit to hunt" with all its privileges and responsibilities.

50

The Homecoming:

When All Is Said and Done

"One truth stands firm. All that happens in world history rests on something spiritual. If the spiritual is strong, it creates world history. If it is weak, it suffers world history."

Albert Schweitzer

I would not presume to tell you what to believe in. Nor would I ever mandate a spirit journey path, because each person must be free to choose his or her own direction, his or her own world view.

But I will tell you I believe there has been a spiritual dimension to human existence since we first stood upright and considered ourselves as subject and object. I tell students that they are free to believe in the Spirit, much as they may choose to believe in oxygen. Whether they believe in air or not, it fills their lungs each time they breath. So it is, in my mind, with the Spirit.

Please encourage your student to include things spiritual in their lives just as they would:

Scholarship
Community service
Healthy lifestyle choices
Good nutrition
Love

It can be a part of life that enriches all the others. Do not force them to go to church, synagogue, or mosque, but rather encourage them on their spiritual journey. Trust the Spirit to guide them and light their paths.

Einstein said, "I want to know the mind of God; the rest are just details." Help your student see the presence of the Spirit in secular life, and she or he will be strong against the winds that blow into every life. "They will run and not be weary, they will mount up with wings like eagles."

A Prayer for Parents

Now I lay me down to sleep

I pray the school my child to keep.

Away from harm and into books,

A friend to all, no dirty looks.

I love her so, he is my life,

I hope for learning, and little strife.

My vivid mortality, now I see;

Like birds, my children, they now fly free.

Their own great journey has now begun,

My job, however, is far from done.

I'll write, I'll wonder, I make a quick call,

But for right now, I'll just sit and bawl.

The Spirit giveth, and taketh away,

Would I have it any other way?

One thing I will not fail to do,

And that is to say, "I do love you."

For parents and children and schools everywhere,

I pray for us this rhythmic prayer.

That God be with us and also with them,

My baby, my child, and now my friend.

With love,
Will Keim